Cultivating Habits of the Heart

First Principles of Disciplined Living

by Jeff Reed

A six-session Bible study for small groups

THE | FIRST
PRINCIPLES
S E R I E S   O N E

1

LearnCorp Resources is committed to assisting churches, parents, Christian schools,
and Christian businessmen and women with resources to carry out their prospec-
tive ministries.

These materials are designed to integrate with BILD-International resources, which
are designed to help churches train leaders.

Art direction and design: Bill Thielker

Cover Image: *Cyclopedia of Biblical Theological and Ecclesiastical Literature* by
McClintock and James Strong

All Scripture, unless otherwise noted, is from the New American Standard Bible.

ISBN 1-891441-03-5

1.1

Table of Contents

Cultivating Habits of the Heart / 5

Introduction to the Series / 7

    Today's Fast-Paced Society / 7

    Design of the Series / 8

    Design of the Study Guides / 10

Session 1: Christ Dwelling in Our Hearts / 13

Session 2: Cultivating Habits in Our Individual Lives / 22

Session 3: Cultivating Habits in Our Families / 31

Session 4: Cultivating Habits in Our Church Family / 40

Session 5: Cultivating Habits in Our LifeWork / 50

Session 6: Reshaping Our Lives / 60

Endnotes / 65

Glossary of Key Biblical Terms and Concepts / 66

Lifelong Learning / 68

PREFACE – A Living Story

This series has grown out of the labor of many faithful believers. It has been developed in the context of the ministry of establishing churches for over 25 years. The story of its development is truly a living story, filled with faithful men and women serving Jesus Christ as they build their lives, families, and churches upon these first principles.

A first word of thanks goes to my immediate family. To my wife Nancy, who has taught me the true meaning of faithfulness. To the editing team, which is made up of the three generations of women in my life—Nancy, my mother-in-law Maxine, and my daughter Anna—whose lives truly adorn the gospel. Without this team, the booklets would not be grammatically correct or readable. In addition, thanks to my son Jonathan, who is diligently laboring to make this series live for high school students, and to my son-in-law George Stagg, who has overseen the entire publishing project. Both are emerging as faithful, young ministers of the gospel.

A word of thanks to my church family—Oakwood Road Church (previously known as Ontario Bible Church)—who have endured the endless development of this material over 25 years, beginning with ugly green notebooks. This small, faithful group of believers have built their lives on the first principles of the faith and are now reaping the fruit of their labor in the lives of their children and in a worldwide ministry.

A word of thanks to all the leaders and churches who are part of BILD International's worldwide network, who have faithfully used and contributed to the development of BILD resources from which this series is developed and in which it is designed to be integrated. Already several translation projects have begun to place this series in other languages. Special thanks to Don McReavy, who goaded me into producing the initial *Establishing Series*, and who continues to labor with me in its development.

A word of thanks to my two partners in LearnCorp Resources—Bob Goris and Charlie Stagg. Just as many strategic people helped make the apostle Paul's journeys possible, they have invested significant resources to make this series a reality. In addition, thanks to Bill Thielker, an outstanding designer, who truly seeks to be faithful to the skills and craft that God has entrusted to him.

On behalf of the entire church family listed above, it is our prayer that God will use this series as a modern day didache—or catechism if you will—to help establish tens of thousands, if not hundreds of thousands, in the first principles of the faith, that their churches might multiply and their families produce fruit for generations to come.

Jeff Reed

October, 1997

Cultivating Habits of the Heart — Introduction

One of the most significant books written on American culture in the last twenty years is entitled *Habits of the Heart: Individualism and Commitment in American Life.* This book has contributed to a rigorous scholarly and popular debate. The essence of its message is simply this: American individualism has undermined community disciplines and commitments to the degree that an integrated, healthy culture is at risk. The *habits of the heart,* they reason, are a set of disciplines that far supercede an individual's development; they include an integrated set of family and community disciplines as well. Yet, these family and community habits of the heart are becoming almost foreign to the selfish and individualistic pursuits of the average American. While this sociological cultural study provides significant insights, it cannot begin to provide the comprehensive answers that we have at our fingertips as disciples of Jesus Christ.

Yet, it seems that much of Christianity in the West has succumbed to this same individualistic spirit. Much of our contemporary discipleship material focuses on habits of the individual, with little attention given to family and community habits. We are called to spend time with God—often called *devotions, quiet times, time in the Word,* etc.—with a high degree of disciplined habit. There is almost no corresponding level of "habits" challenged in our other spheres of life. Even further removed is a call to integrate a comprehensive set of individual, family, church family, and work habits. We place our individual pursuits, even our spiritual habits, far ahead of those of family and community life.

In this booklet, we will take a radically different approach to the *habits of the heart.* God never intended our lives to be based on a set of individual daily habits, but rather on a whole life orientation that grows out of family and community life. We are not to gain insights from the Word fundamentally in isolation but from disciplines in all spheres of our lives. God carefully designed these habits to guide our lives so that Christ can richly dwell in our hearts, resulting in our entire lives being transformed by our calling. In session one, we will develop an understanding of what it means for Christ to dwell in our hearts, along with an orientation of having our hearts firmly rooted in the faith. In sessions two through five, we will examine the habits of the heart that we need to cultivate in each area of our lives. We will focus first, in session two, on habits in our individual lives—habits that need to be part of our personal growth in the faith and in our relationship with God. These habits are foundational to maturing in Christ, but when they are developed in isolation from family and community disciplines, they become significantly distorted. We will then focus, in session three, on cultivating habits in our family lives. These habits are essential both to passing on our faith to our children as well as to building solid, biblical marriages and intergenerational heritage. In session four, we will focus on cultivating habits in our church family that are essential for the sound and mature development of our faith. One of the most significant reasons that sincere believers fail to be properly and soundly established in their faith is that they fail to develop these church-family community habits. Finally in session five, we will focus on what we are calling *lifework habits*—habits that integrate our faith into our everyday lives in the world around us. In essence, developing serious, integrated life habits is really nothing more than bringing every area of our lives under discipline—the discipline required of a disciple of Jesus Christ.

As in all of the other booklets, session six is designed to pull it all together. This is especially helpful in this book, since its very intent is to build an integrated set of life habits. It is designed to move the knowledge we have learned in the first three booklets fully into our hearts, that we might completely grasp (and therefore fully live) the magnificent plan that God has set before our lives and families. Session six goes a long way in integrating all of our work from the first four books of series one of *The First Principles Series*.

So let's begin this very critical task of cultivating a set of lifelong *habits of the heart*, that we might become firmly established in our faith; transformed in our inner man; and fully grasp, with those believers around us, "the breadth and length and height and depth" of the love of Christ and His plan for the ages.

THE FIRST PRINCIPLES SERIES

The Demands of Today's Fast-Paced Society

We are entering a whole new way of life—computers, endless streams of information, new work realities—that demands continuous learning. This environment puts tremendous pressure on our time, finances, and relationships.

As Christians, we are under even more pressure. Besides making a living in this society and doing a good job in our homes and marriages, there is the extra desire to serve God, which includes having an effective ministry. Students have to juggle assignments, work hours, and family involvement, as well as involvement in a local church and the tremendous opportunity for ministry among peers. This involves more time and resources—at home, in the workplace, at school, and directly in the life of the local church community. There seems to be little time for one's own personal growth and development.

Our culture builds into us a mindset about so many things, one of which is our personal development.

We want quick fixes—not long-term solutions.

We want how to's—not the ability to think clearly.

We want short training—not lifelong learning.

We want tantalizing subjects—not serious ordered learning.

We want fill-in-the-blank exercises—not reflective writing.

We want one-time applications—not serious projects.

If we are going to be effective as Christians in the 21st century, we must carve out regular time for personal growth and development. This cannot be neglected if we expect significant fruit to come from our lives. We must have some sort of strategy that will help guide us lifelong. And we must take the first step.

The First Principles Series is designed to be just such a first step.

Design of The First Principles Series I-III

This booklet is part of a set of four booklets, which make up Series I. The whole collection, Series I-III, totals thirteen booklets. They are all built around an idea found in Paul's letter to the church at Colossae written almost 2000 years ago.

> See to it that no one takes you captive through philosophy and empty deception, according to the tradition of men, according to the elementary principles of the world, rather than according to Christ. (Colossians 2:8)

The phrase *the elementary principles* is best translated "the first principles." They are the basic fundamentals of the faith. They represent the first things that must be learned, upon which everything else is built. If they are not carefully understood, everything else will be distorted. The writer of the letter to the Hebrews understood this when he exhorted the Hebrew Christians who were forgetting their newfound faith, in Hebrews 5:

> 11) Concerning him we have much to say, and *it is* hard to explain, since you have become dull of hearing. 12) For though by this time you ought to be teachers, you have need again for someone to teach you the elementary principles of the oracles of God, and you have come to need milk and not solid food. 13) For everyone who partakes only of milk is not accustomed to the word of righteousness, for he is a babe. 14) But solid food is for the mature, who because of practice have their senses trained to discern good and evil.

The Hebrew Christians forgot the first principles of their faith. Once they became Christians, their Jewish family members and friends put tremendous pressure on them to return to Judaism and began challenging the basics of the Christian faith. It is clear from this passage that it is impossible to move on toward maturity without carefully understanding the first principles.

This series of booklets is designed to lead you through the first principles so that you can build upon them and grow on toward maturity. In every generation of churches since the time of the New Testament, believers were expected to learn these first principles. In the early church, before new believers were accepted into the church, they needed to learn *the didache* ("the teaching"). "The Didache" was a summary of the basic teaching of the New Testament—the first principles. During the Reformation (1500's), this teaching was called *catechism*, again designed to help Christians master the first principles.

Actually, the concept of *first principles* is important in every area of life. It is central to all quality education. Almost 150 years ago, in the classic work *The Idea of the University*, John Newman referred to a concept he called "pushing up the first principles." According to Newman, the purpose of a university is to teach the first principles of every discipline and then to explore the full limits of those first principles—pushing the principles up through all levels of research.

So it is with our Christian faith. Once we have mastered the first principles, we are able to push them up through all areas of our lives. That is, we are ready to move on to maturity. *The First Principles Series* is carefully designed to help you lay the foundation of your faith.

Whether you are a new believer, a believer who needs to have these first principles laid carefully for the first time, or for whatever reason you need to have them laid afresh, do your work carefully and you will reap a lifetime of benefits.

The First Principles

Series I

1. Becoming a Disciple
   First Principles of the Faith

2. Belonging to a Family of Families
   First Principles of Community Life

3. Participating in the Mission of the Church
   First Principles of Community Purpose

4. Cultivating Habits of the Heart
   First Principles of Disciplined Living

Series II

1. Enjoying Your Relationship
   First Principles of Marriage

2. Passing on Your Beliefs
   First Principles of Family Life

3. Envisioning Fruitful LifeWork
   First Principles of Ministry

4. Building for Future Generations
   First Principles of True Success

Series III

1. Handling the Word with Confidence
   First Principles of Bible Study

2. Unfolding the Great Commission
   First Principles from Acts

3. Laying Solid Foundations in the Gospel
   First Principles from 1 & 2 Thessalonians

4. Catching God's Vision for the Church
   First Principles from Ephesians

5. Living in God's Household
   First Principles from the Pastorals

Design of the Study Guides

This series is designed to lead you through a learning process—a process designed to teach you to think. This process is based upon the Hebrew wisdom model in the Bible (the Bible's educational literature) and on sound, contemporary, educational research. It is used in all of LearnCorp's Bible studies, so once you have mastered the process it will serve you for all of your future work in these and subsequent series. It will also provide a natural study model that you can apply to all areas of your life.

The first five weeks, you will follow a four-step study process. The sixth week is a summary session and final step. You will "pull together" all of your work from the first five weeks into a final project and share it in your small group.

Consistent Study Process (CSP)

A Consistent Study Process (CSP) is used in these books to take you through a complete learning cycle every time you study a passage or concept in the Scriptures. CSP can also serve as a convenient reminder that Bible study is not ESP—we are not trying to mystically experience the text, but to carefully and soundly study the text. There are four basic steps to this process and one final step that integrates the work from the first four.

The First Five Weeks: In the first five sessions of every First Principles study guide, the four basic steps will be done each week: (1) Study the Scriptures, (2) Consult the Scholars, (3) Think Through the Issues, and (4) Apply the Principles.

The importance of each step is explained below.

Study the Scriptures

This step is foundational. We cannot begin exploring the issues of the Bible without first understanding exactly what the passages mean. Discussion groups in which everyone simply shares his opinion are disrespectful of the Scriptures, and therefore to God. They are often merely a pooling of ignorance.

You will go through this same first step in every session, in every booklet. You will begin with a passage to read, answer a few basic questions about the passage, and finally summarize the core teaching of the passage.

Your work in this step:
- Read the passage.
- Think through the questions.
- Summarize the core teaching of the passage.

Consult the Scholars

This step is very important as well, although it is not always highly valued by Christians in our generation. God raises up teachers and scholars to serve in every generation. These teachers can do great harm or great good to churches. We have provided you with some solid, carefully chosen research—in nugget form—to stimulate your thinking. These nuggets of research take two forms. One is a brief commentary on the passage. The other consists of several short instructional quotes on the ideas related to the core truths of the passage.

Your work in this step:
- Read and reflect on the brief commentary.
- Read and reflect on the key quotes.
- Record any insights from the readings.

Think Through the Issues

This step is designed to help you think through the implications of the core teaching of the passage that you have been studying. Unless we go through this process, we can gloss over the significance of the core truths—the first principles of the faith. This is best done in a small group where issues can be discussed thoroughly. Debate an issue in light of the biblical text and try to come to one conclusion as a group. It is not a time for airing opinions but for genuine interaction with the issues.

Your work in this step:
- Think through the issue before discussion.
- Record your initial thoughts on the issue before discussion.
- Discuss the issue in your small group.
- Record your final thoughts after the discussion.

Apply the Principles

This step brings the basic learning cycle to completion. It is not enough to gain a clear grasp of an issue. It is not enough to accurately understand the core truths of a passage or verse in the Bible. We must apply it to our lives. Applications should be specific and related to the core truths of the passages studied.

Your work in this step:
- Think back through the first three steps.
- Design an application for your life.

The Sixth Week: The last session in the study guide is the final step.

Reshaping Our Lives

This step brings together the entire study process. In each of the first five weeks, we moved through the 4-step Consistent Study Process (CSP). Now in the sixth week, you will pull together all of your work and evaluate your whole life.

Too often today, we stop short of what is necessary to really change our lives. Thinking through simple applications is very important as we study the Bible, but thinking through our whole lives in light of these new truths is essential. The final step in the study process requires that we rethink our entire lives in light of the truths we have been studying—that we rearrange our worldview. We must allow the truths to reshape every aspect of our lives.

Your work in this step:
- Commit your heart—by reflection, personal journaling, and prayer.
- Commit your mind—by forming clear convictions and memorizing Scripture.
- Commit your life—by decisions, personal projects, and life habits.

Two Final Parts of the Study Guides: Each study booklet contains two additional parts—a glossary and a lifelong learning section.

Glossary of Key Biblical Terms and Concepts—The glossary is designed to help you with important terms that you may have encountered for the first time in your study. They are kept to a minimum in the guides, but it is not possible or preferable to remove all terms with special meaning. New terms—especially biblical terms full of rich truths—just have to be learned. To make this process easier, we have included a glossary.

Lifelong Learning—This final section introduces you to additional resources that you may want to pursue. After completing a study guide, it is crucial that you do not view yourself as finished. You must understand that you are laying foundations for a lifetime of learning. Several resources are recommended for your further development.

CHRIST DWELLING IN OUR HEARTS

SESSION 1

Now that we understand the essence of the first principles of our faith from studying the first three booklets, how can we be confident that we are moving this new knowledge from our heads to our hearts? It is obviously not enough to intellectually understand the essentials of our faith and the overall plan of God. We must allow them to penetrate deeply into our hearts and to begin transforming every aspect of our lives. We must begin to grasp the full significance of what it means to be a Christian—a disciple—and let that begin to encompass our every desire. In Ephesians 3:14-21, Paul prayed this very thing for the church at Ephesus. He prayed that the full implications of God's magnificent calling on their lives would actually dwell in their hearts. And as a result, that they might fully comprehend all that God had for them. Let's study this passage to gain some insight into embedding the faith in our hearts.

 Study the Scriptures

Read the Passage: Ephesians 3:14-21

Think Through the Questions:

1. What exactly did Paul pray for the church at Ephesus?
2. What did he pray that they would comprehend and what did he hope would result from this full comprehension?
3. In this context, what does it mean "that Christ may dwell in your hearts"?
4. What role do you think Paul saw prayer playing in seeing believers become rooted in their faith?

Summarize the Core Teaching of the Passage:

Write a paragraph, outline, annotate, or chart your conclusions—whatever best communicates for you. Try to summarize the essence of Paul's prayer request for the church at Ephesus. What did he really want to see happen in their lives?

Core teaching of Ephesians 3:14-21:

Consult the Scholars

The following comments are designed to help you better understand the passage and to stimulate your thinking on the implications of the teaching.

Read and Reflect on this Brief Commentary on Ephesians 3:14-21:

It is important to understand the context of Paul's prayer for the church at Ephesus. It is actually the second of two major prayers in his letter. Both prayers are for similar things, and both are positioned in the first section of the letter. When studied in their contexts, it is clear that they are complementary and almost symmetrically placed within the section. They appear in a section of the letter where Paul is giving the Ephesians a fairly complete description of their calling as Christians: what happened to them once they became Christians, what God generally expects from their lives, and a picture of Christ's magnificent plan for His church.

The two prayers, 1:15-23 and 3:14-21, carry a similar concern. Paul wanted them to fully grasp what had happened to them. Notice the phrases he used:

"a spirit of wisdom and of revelation in the knowledge of Him" 1:17

"that the eyes of your heart may be enlightened" 1:18

"that you . . . may be able to comprehend with all of the saints" 3:18

In the midst of his comprehensive explanation of what Christ had done and what He is doing in the world, Paul asked very specifically for them to have a real heart-level understanding. Notice *heart* is used twice: the "eyes of your heart," and that Christ may "dwell in your hearts." But he also attached concepts such as *knowledge, comprehension,* and *enlightenment.* Notice that the dwelling of Christ in their hearts was not primarily an experience, but a full grasping of the revelation—of the teaching, of the truth—in a way that pervaded their hearts and literally overwhelmed them. It was an inner transformation ("inner man," see 3:16). This is very different from Eastern religion's concept of enlightenment, which empties one's mind of everything in order to get in touch with creation around. It is also very different from The Enlightenment—a historical era in the West that is based on scientific discovery. And it is quite different from the common Christian practice of "enlightenment" in the form of morning devotions. This is when we are enlightened from a verse that "speaks personally" to us, although the insight may be very different from what the author intended to say.

What is the content of this revelation that is to overwhelm us? Specifically, according to Ephesians chapters 1-3, Christ has a magnificent plan for all of eternity, and we are part of it. He is building His church, His temple, and eventually His kingdom. All the true riches of the universe belong to Him, and we are now part of it. Our sins are forgiven, and we are now heirs of all that is His. It is just as if we are already sitting on the throne with Him. On top of this, He has given us good works to accomplish while on this earth. He will use our lives and His churches to accomplish His purposes as He builds His church.

So what does it mean to be enlightened? And how does it happen? What is the role of prayer? What is the work of the Spirit? What is the role of the revelation itself? It is clear from this text that the enlightenment was content-based. It was revelation, not just an experience. Those who were trying to establish the believers fully in their faith prayed that they would really grasp what had happened to them; in this case, Paul was doing the praying. It also appears that the Spirit of God was at work in their hearts and minds, enabling them to fully grasp these realities. And it appears that the revelation, Paul's prayer, and the work of the Spirit were intended to cause their hearts to be overwhelmed by the reality of all that Christ had done for them and was doing for them, that He might dwell (completely reside) in their hearts (the core of one's being and life aspirations).

You see, our relationship with Christ is not primarily a personal experience based on faithfully applying a few daily habits. It is not a daily, almost mystical, enlightenment from a verse of Scripture, which depends on our faithful 15-minute spurts of discipline. It is primarily a heart that is overwhelmed by comprehending what Christ has done and is doing, followed by the wise and disciplined conduct (habits) of our lives, which is based upon that revelation. This calls for a set of *habits of the heart* that cover every area of our lives, or "walk" as Paul calls it in his transitional verse in 4:1. We are to fully grasp Christ's revelation and build our entire lives around it. These disciplines that we build in every area of our lives are what we are calling the *habits of the heart*. (The entire letter to the Ephesians will be studied much more in-depth in Series Three, book four.)

Read and Reflect on Key Quotes:

The following quote is taken from *Riches in Christ* by Ray Stedman, a book built around a series of sermons by Stedman on Ephesians 1-3. Stedman was one of the most influential church renewal writers and teachers in the 60's, 70's, and 80's. His most famous book, *Body Life*, is becoming a classic. This quote is a commentary on Ephesians 3:18.

"I want to stress that we are not to live in isolation—that is our problem—but to relate to one another, to 'realize with all saints,' and not to try to work things out all alone. . . . As we begin to relate to and to share with one another, then we begin to realize the height and depth and length and breadth.

"What does he mean? There are many who have made beautiful suggestions about the meaning of these four dimensions. Some see in them the cross, with its height and depth and length and breadth. Some see them as a description of the love of God. But I think they are a reference to some of the things Paul has already talked about in this letter. The 'length' is what he calls in chapter 1 'the hope to which you are called'—that hope which began before the foundation of the world, in eternity past, and reaches on through all of recorded time into the unsearchable, limitless reaches of eternity yet to come. That is the length and scope of God's program. We are caught up in God's vast, cosmic endeavor to bring all things together in Christ. That is the hope to which we are called.

"The 'breadth' is what he refers to as 'the riches of his inheritance among the Gentiles'—the fact that Jews and Gentiles and all men alike are gathered up in the church, without difference or division—black, white, rich, poor, slave, freeman, male, female—it doesn't make any difference. All are one, sharing equally in the riches of Jesus Christ, through the cross.

"The 'height' indicates where we are in Christ—risen to sit together with Him in heavenly places, far above all principalities, all powers, all authorities, in this age and in the age to come. It is the place of authority as a Christian, the place of power to be freed from everything that would drag us down, and to live above all that would twist and demolish and destroy in our lives.

"And finally, the 'depth' is what he has described in chapter 2 as death, the living death out of which God has called us. In that death we were victims instead of victors, following the course of this age, living unwittingly as directed by the prince of the power of the air, following the passions of the flesh, doing what we thought was right and ending up being wrong in everything we attempted. We were 'children of wrath,' as Paul described us—'by nature children of wrath like the rest of mankind.' Out of that living death—the depths of human depravity—God called us into the heights with Christ."[1]

Record any insights from the brief commentary and quotes:

_____

_____

_____

_____

_____

_____

_____

_____

_____

_____

_____

_____

_____

_____

_____

_____

_____

_____

_____

_____

_____

Think Through the Issues

When we first learn something, it is easy to be excited, yet to fall far short of fully comprehending the significance of what we have learned. This being the case, it follows that the new knowledge will not affect our lives at the level that it could and will lose its transforming effect. Paul's prayer in Ephesians 3:14-21 was that the Ephesians would fully comprehend their faith and, as a result, that Christ and His plans and purposes would dwell in their hearts, thus overwhelming and consuming their lives. What is involved in this full comprehension?

Issue: Fully comprehending the faith

Think Through the Issue Before Discussion:

1. Why is it important to fully comprehend our faith?

2. What might be some indications that we do not fully comprehend our faith? That the principles are not fully impacting our lives?

3. What would be some early signs that Christ is actually beginning to dwell in our hearts?

4. What sort of life—or heart—habits would seem to be part of a process of "comprehending with all the saints" the depths of our new life in Christ? What do "all the saints" have to do with the habits?

Record your initial thoughts on the issue before discussion:

Discuss the issue in your small group.

Record your final thoughts on the issue after discussion:

Apply the Principles

It is now time to respond to what you have studied and discussed. Take your time on this section.

Think Back Through the First Three Steps.

At this stage in the series, it is crucial to reflect on how much impact the first principles are having in your life as a whole. Are you being highly impacted and beginning to comprehend the all-encompassing significance of the work of God in your life? Is it starting to take up residence in your heart?

Design an Application for Your Life.

Complete the assigned project, and record any additional applications. There are two aspects to this project. The first is to design a personal prayer for your life like Paul's prayers for the Ephesians. Ask God to give you full comprehension of your calling and that Christ may begin to dwell in your heart, that is, that His plans and purposes will captivate your entire life. Then make a list of some initial life habits—*habits of the heart*—that you need to develop to fully comprehend and internalize Christ's plan for your life.

Design a personal prayer for your life, based on Paul's example. Then list a few habits of the heart that you need in order to grow in your comprehension of Christ and His purposes.

CULTIVATING HABITS IN OUR INDIVIDUAL LIVES
SESSION 2

When we think of defining a core set of habits for our personal lives, we have to begin by focusing on the Word. We cannot expect Christ to dwell in our hearts if our hearts are twisted and distorted by other goals and aspirations. The only reliable source for dividing "the thoughts and intentions of our heart" is the Word of God, the Scriptures (Hebrews 4:12). To focus on our hearts, we must begin by renewing our minds, as we studied in session four of *Becoming a Disciple*. This renewing process involves a core set of habits by which we focus our lives. However, as you will see as we move through this booklet, the habits of the heart of a disciple are far more than a small set of personal habits; in fact, even the personal habits have a very important corporate element to them. In the passage in this session, Colossians 3:1-17, we will focus on the foundations of the heart of a disciple. We will see how to begin to focus our whole lives around Christ and His purposes—what Paul called "putting on the new self."

 ## Study the Scriptures

Read the Passage: Colossians 3:1-17

Think Through the Questions:

1. What does it mean to "set your mind on the things above"? How exactly do we begin to do that?

2. What does it mean "to put on the new self"? Again, how do we go about doing that?

3. What role does the Word seem to play in focusing our hearts on the things above? What does it mean for the Word to "richly dwell within you"?

4. Is allowing the Word to richly dwell in our lives primarily an individual, personal matter? What role does the community of faith play in focusing our minds on Christ and His purposes?

Summarize the Core Teaching of the Passage:

Write a paragraph, outline, annotate, or chart your conclusions—whatever best communicates for you. Be sure to comment specifically on how to go about focusing your mind on the things above and letting the Word permeate your heart.

Core teaching of Colossians 3:1-17:

Consult the Scholars

The following comments are designed to help you better understand the passage and to stimulate your thinking on the implications of the teaching.

Read and Reflect on this Brief Commentary on Colossians 3:1-17:

Colossians 3:1-17 is one of the richest (and clearest) passages within Paul's letters that addresses the personal focus of our lives. It gives a rather complete picture of the inner transformation that needs to take place in our lives. Both our minds and our hearts are addressed in this passage. Moreover, the focus is broader than just a set of instructions concerning our individual habits. It extends to the role of the local church community in helping us develop necessary heart habits that insure the permeation of the first principles of the faith into our minds and hearts—and thus into our entire lives. Before commenting on the passage, though, let's take a moment to place this section in the context of Paul's complete letter to the church at Colossae.

Just as in his letter to the Ephesians, Paul first majored on Christ's administration, His church, and all that these new believers had as Christians—an inheritance for all eternity with Christ. Then, beginning in 2:6, he focused on their walk—their new lifestyle (way of living) that was to accompany their inheritance. He first built his argument concerning their walk around two sets of principles: the principles of the world and the principles of Christ. He used the concept of *elementary principles* (the term literally means "first principles"—again, the idea this series of booklets is based upon) to encase his argument, in 2:8 and 2:20. Essentially, his point is this: There are generally two sets of principles in life—the world's and Christ's. Therefore, at one level, all of man's philosophies share a similar man-centered focus. The principles of the world focus on self-made religions by self-made men. Their life focus is here—on this earth and all that man can make and do. Not so the principles of Christ.

Now let's turn to 3:1-17. What is the message here? Essentially it addresses the new lifestyle of believers in Christ—a new lifestyle (way of life, habit of life) built upon the first principles of Christ. He addresses the family lifestyle in another "household text" beginning in 3:18. But first he addresses the individual lives of these new believers at the church at Colossae. What does he say about this new lifestyle? It is a life of Christ—like Christ. The core of his description of this life is one of others, not self. We are not to serve ourselves—our flesh—but Christ. This means that we are to develop a change within ourselves, putting on a heart of compassion, forgiveness, humility, etc., that is, a heart of love. And whatever we do, we are to do it to the glory of God. The change is to be internal—a change in our hearts. And it is spoken of as an inner renewal that we are all to experience.

Now what does the passage say about this personal inner renewal? The passage is framed with three interesting phrases: one near the beginning, one in the middle, and one near the end. First he says to "set your mind on the things above, not on the things that are on earth," 3:2. That is, focus on the first principles of Christ, not on the first principles of the world. The Greek word for "set your mind on" speaks of our whole mindset, life attitude, frame of mind—literally our whole attitude toward life. How we think about life and how we think through the issues of life are to grow out of the philosophy of Christ, not out of the philosophy of the world. Our whole lives are to be built upon the first principles of Christ. Second, we are "being renewed to a true knowledge," 3:10. Our heart change is not primarily based on experience, but upon true knowledge. Not on some clever philosophy or religion, but it is based on the true philosophy (first principles) of Christ. The final phrase is in 3:16, "Let the word of Christ richly dwell within you." Notice several things about this phrase. The word of Christ is to dwell in us. In this context, the foundation is the first principles of Christ. By "richly dwell," it implies that we are to be saturated in this philosophy, in these principles of Christ. We are to build on them. We are to understand them from every angle. We are to teach them; correct each other by them; and to meditate, creating psalms and hymns (possibly a little poetry!); and even to sing them to each other. Note the words "one another"—the principles richly dwell in us in the context of the life of the church community.

So, in essence, what habits of the heart are described in this passage? It describes the habit of building our inner lives upon the philosophy, or first principles, of Christ. We are to be saturated by them. We are to master them—teaching and correcting our lives by them, letting them shape our whole mindset toward life. We are to meditate on them, even to the extent of turning them into hymns and songs. In addition, we are to turn our private study and meditation into community sharing. This implies that our inner renewal from the word of Christ takes place in community. We learn from each other. The word of Christ dwells in our lives at its fullest when we live and learn with a community of believers.

Read and Reflect on Key Quotes:

Again, it is appropriate to turn to Francis Schaeffer, one of the clearest thinkers of the 21st century. In this quote taken from *True Spirituality*, he focuses on the powerful world of ideas—biblical ideas—and their effect on the reality of loving God with our hearts.

"First of all, we must understand that the reality of communion with God, and loving God, must take place in the inward self. There is no use talking about loving God except to understand that it takes place in the inward world of our thoughts. Even communication with men and women must be through the body into the area of the thought-world. If a man and a woman have only an external contact, this cannot be called 'communication.' It is only mechanical. But a real, personal communication never remains external. It always goes back into the personality. This is true in the area of married life, the man-woman relationship as God meant it to be. Merely to have physical contact is not communication on a personal level. This must flow back into the area of personality. Only then it can be called communication. Thus real communication with man and love of man centers in our thought-world. The results may be external and the expression is external, but the love is internal. The same is true in our love for God. The result can be external, but love itself is always internal. If Christians can only learn this, very many problems concerning the Christian life would assume a different perspective. Let us understand how important is the world of thoughts. It is this that distinguishes me as a man, in contrast to machines. This is what I am, and my calling is to love God with all my heart and soul and mind.

"The second conclusion is that the real battle for men is in the world of ideas, rather than in that which is outward. All heresy, for example, begins in the world of ideas. That is why, when new workers come to L'Abri, we always stress to them that we are interested in ideas rather than personalities or organizations. Ideas are to be discussed, not personalities or organizations. Ideas are the stock of the thought-world, and from the ideas burst forth all the external things: painting, music, buildings, the love and the hating of men in practice, and equally the results of loving God or rebellion against God, in the external world. Where a man will spend eternity depends on his reading or hearing the ideas, the propositional truth, the facts of the gospel in the external world, and these being carried through the medium of his body into the inner world of his thoughts, and there, inside himself, in his thought-world, either his believing God on the basis of the content of the gospel or his calling God a liar. This is not merely a mystical, existentialist experience. It is not the 'final experience' of a man like Carl Jaspers put in religious terms; it is not the hallucinatory drug experience, without content. It can be expressed rationally. It is ideas, it is the content of the good news. But as far as what it means to a man is concerned, it is whether he accepts it or rejects it in the thought-world that makes the difference: if he believes God, or if he calls Him a liar.

"It is for this reason that the preaching of the gospel can never be primarily a matter of organization. The preaching of the gospel is ideas, flaming ideas brought to men, as God has revealed them to us in Scripture. It is not a contentless experience internally received, but it is contentful ideas internally acted upon that makes the difference. So when we state our doctrines, they must be ideas, and not just phrases. We cannot use doctrines as though they were mechanical pieces to a puzzle. True doctrine is an idea revealed by God in the Bible and an idea that fits properly into the external world as it is, and as God made it, and to man as he is, as God made him, and can be fed back through man's body into his thought-world and there acted upon. The battle for man is centrally in the world of thought.

"The third conclusion, and the shortest of the three is that the Christian life, true spirituality, always begins inside, in our thought-world. All that has been said in our earlier study of being free in this present life from the bonds of sin, and also of being free in the present life from the results of the bonds of sin, is meaningless jargon, no more than a psychological pill, without the reality that God thinks and we think, and that at each step the internal is central and first. The spiritual battle, the loss or victory, is always in the thought-world. [2]

Record any insights from the brief commentary and quotes:

Think Through the Issues

In our culture today, we tend to define everything by our personal experience. Truth is beyond our reach. Most of us view life as a collective set of personal opinions. Yet, this is not the way of a disciple of Jesus Christ. We are to cultivate a frame of mind, a philosophy, that is to completely transform our lives and lifestyles. This transformation, based upon the first principles of Christ, is cultivated by a set of habits. Think through what it would really take, day in and day out, to form such a life focus.

Issue: Habitually setting our minds and hearts (our lives) on Christ and on the things of Christ

Think Through the Issue Before Discussion:

1. What does it really take to set your mind on the things of Christ? To be renewed according to the true knowledge? What all is involved?

2. What are the core ingredients of habitually dwelling on the word of Christ? Which habits seem to be individual, and which ones involve the life of the church community?

3. What kind of time do you think would be required to take these habits seriously in your life?

Record your initial thoughts on the issue before discussion:

Discuss the issue in your small group.

Record your final thoughts on the issue after discussion:

Apply the Principles

It is now time to respond to what you have studied and discussed. Take your time on this section.

Think Back Through the First Three Steps.

Design an Application for Your Life.

Evaluate your lifestyle. Purpose to build a mindset—a life philosophy—completely focused on the things of Christ. Begin by evaluating the current focuses of your life. Then sketch out a core set of personal life habits that would drench you in the things of Christ. Put time commitments to these habits.

Record personal habits of the heart and any accompanying time commitments to these habits:

CULTIVATING HABITS IN OUR FAMILIES
SESSION 3

When addressing the concept of internalizing the first principles—cultivating habits leading to a fully Christian lifestyle—we can not just focus on our individual life habits. The first principles of the faith call for a disciplined lifestyle in every sphere of our lives. One of these spheres is family life. It, too, must be disciplined by the first principles of the faith. Often people think of their faith as a personal issue and fail to integrate their faith fully into their family lives. In this session we will focus on habits needed in our families, with special attention given to training our children in the faith, a process that requires its own set of habits of the heart. We will focus our attention on Ephesians 6:1-4, which instructs us on habits of a household. In our culture, our work often takes so much out of us that we can, and usually do, neglect these family habits. We must learn to habitually orient our families around these principles.

 Study the Scriptures

Read the Passage: Ephesians 6:1-4

Think Through the Questions:

1. Who is primarily responsible for laying the foundation of the faith in children?

2. What is the difference between "discipline" and "instruction"?

3. Why do you think there is a warning to fathers not to provoke their children to anger?

4. What is involved in honoring our parents? What does this have to do with living long on the earth?

Summarize the Core Teaching of the Passage:

Write a paragraph, outline, annotate, or chart your conclusions—whatever best communicates for you. Be sure to comment on the difference between discipline and instruction, as well as your thoughts on the commitment required in this exhortation.

Core teaching of Ephesians 6:1-4:

_____

_____

_____

_____

_____

_____

_____

_____

_____

_____

_____

_____

_____

_____

_____

_____

_____

_____

_____

_____

_____

_____

Consult the Scholars

The following comments are designed to help you better understand the passage and to stimulate your thinking about the implications of the teaching.

Read and Reflect on this Brief Commentary on Ephesians 6:1-4:

This is part of one of the basic household texts on the family. Its parallel passage is Colossians 3:20-21, which is also part of a household text. We already established the context of the book of Ephesians in

Belonging to a Family of Families (see pages 14-15), and we will deal with this text more completely in book two of the next series. Our focus here is on one particular aspect of this household text—the foundational disciplines of the Christian family and the accompanying habits of the heart required to put the instructions fully into action.

The core disciplines are given in 4:4, centering on the words "discipline and instruction," which we will examine in a moment. But first note that the command to carry out this discipline and instruction of the children is given to fathers. The father is to take the lead in the training, though both parents are clearly involved, since the children are commanded to obey their parents in 4:1. The basic idea is that the children are to obey the discipline and instruction of their parents, all conducted under the authority and leadership of the father. This concept is pictured beautifully in the book of Proverbs in the Old Testament. Proverbs 1:8 calls for the son to listen to his "father's instruction" (teaching with authority) and his "mother's teaching" (a general word for basic teaching). The reality of the influence of a mother and father is visualized metaphorically by Paul in 1 Thessalonians 2, where he described his training of the young churches. He stated that he was gentle with them like a mother and exhorting and encouraging like a father. Fathers are given a special warning, which again emphasizes that they have the primary responsibility. They are not to use their authority in a way that exasperates their children, but they are responsible to shape their children's lives.

Two specific words are used by Paul to describe the training process: "discipline and instruction." The first word *discipline* (literally "paideia," a common word used even today for good overall education) referred in Paul's day to the general upbringing attained by discipline. The word for *instruction* literally means "to place in mind," in other words, to teach them how to think (frame of mind), along with an admonition to follow the teaching. The admonition seems to cover the entire training process. However, the sphere is narrowed to the discipline and instruction "of the Lord." The context again calls forth the idea of the first principles. The first principles of the faith are to be taught by the parents in a disciplined manner, with the father clearly seeing that the children's lives are shaped around these principles.

Parents need to see that their children are taught the first principles of the faith and that they "push up those principles" into all areas of their general education. (See Newman's concept of the University in the introduction to this series on page 9.) We need to train our children to think through all areas and disciplines of education, based on the first principles, before leaving home. Parents are essentially responsible for an 18+-year discipline—clearly a habit of the heart. This habit is visualized in Deuteronomy 6:6, which is the central and parallel passage for parenting. It exhorts parents to have God's words on their hearts and to teach them to their children when they sit in the house, when they go to bed and get up, and when they go about the affairs of everyday life. Clearly, we are to cultivate this very extensive habit of the heart in our Christian homes.

Read and Reflect on Key Quotes:

The following quote is taken from Stephen B. Clark's insightful work, *Man and Woman in Christ: An Examination of the Roles of Men and Women in Light of Scripture and the Social Sciences*, which deals with all aspects of the household texts on both the family and the church. Here he looks more closely at Ephesians 6:4.

"Contemporary parents often think of their childrearing responsibilities in terms of pre-school training. When children reach age five to six, parents then turn them over to schools and other social institutions for the bulk of their formation and training. New Testament childrearing practices differed drastically from this model. The parents were expected to raise the children to become mature adult Christian men and women. This is the reason for the concern expressed in 1 Timothy 3 and Titus 1 that a man be able to raise his children well. This is also the context for accurately understanding the instruction in Eph. 6:4:

Fathers, do not provoke your children to anger, but bring them up in the discipline and instruction of the Lord.

"The term 'discipline' (*paideia*) in this passage is particularly significant. The word could also be translated 'training,' 'instruction,' 'punishment,' or even 'formation.' The Hebrew equivalent (*musar*) appears often in the wisdom literature of the Old Testament. 'Training' is perhaps a better translation than 'discipline' in this context, because discipline of children in English almost always refers to punishment. Although punishment plays a role in *musar-paideia*, the concept is broader. 'Training' in the scriptural sense is an educational activity which changes the way a person lives. It does not mean only knowledge or mental understanding. It means training to act in a certain way. Moreover, the teaching a person receives when he is trained in the scriptural sense is authoritative teaching backed up by punishment. The trainer bears responsibility for how people turn out. He does not just provide them with ideas and let them do with those ideas as they will. He forms them as people."[3]

Record any insights from the brief commentary and quotes:

Think Through the Issues

Today as Christians, we often do not take our responsibility to train our children seriously. Our homes lack order and discipline, let alone a carefully constructed set of habits of the heart. We are so busy that even traditional family mealtimes have gone by the wayside. We have all seen studies that the average American father spends six minutes a day with his children. Even when we do get serious about the spiritual and moral development of our children, we do not significantly alter the habits of our family lives but rather rely on Sunday school or Christian schools. One of the most alarming trends is that a majority of our children, some figures as high as 60-70%, are not continuing in the faith. In this issue, we will reflect on the vital habits of the heart needed in our Christian families to build solidly on the first principles of the faith.

Issue: The importance of disciplined family habits of the heart

Think Through the Issue Before Discussion:

1. How would you describe the habits of your family life? Is there a clear set of habits and patterns designed to shape the lives of every family member around the first principles of the faith?

2. What sorts of "habits" do you think are needed to thoroughly train your children in the first principles of the faith? Young adults, what habits do you need from your family, in order to be adequately trained?

3. How disciplined do you think you need to be in these habits to be effective?

4. How can extended family members contribute to these habits?

Record your initial thoughts on the issue before discussion:

Discuss the issue in your small group.

Record your final thoughts on the issue after discussion:

Apply the Principles

It is now time to respond to what you have studied and discussed. Take your time on this section.

Think Back Through the First Three Steps.

You may find it difficult to think through the steps of this session, especially if you were not raised in a Christian home. However, if you are to integrate the first principles into your life at every level, it is essential. Give it some time and get creative!

Design an Application for Your Life.

Think through the process of training your children, beginning with the first principles of the faith. What family habits of the heart are needed to train your children? Reading? Stories? Any family dinner activities? Times of family prayer? Any natural habits—walks, bike rides, sports—followed by discussions? Special family traditions? Be creative. Young adults, what family habits of the heart would you like to see happen, both now and in your future families?

A special note to those without children in the home. If you are not yet married or do not have children, you can still identify core habits and envision their future use. If you are single, you can make yourself available to assist families in the church family and in your extended family. Grandparents can contribute a set of grandparenting habits of the heart—letter writing, family traditions, and the use of habits when babysitting or at special visits, etc. Regardless of your station in life, you need to think creatively about the cultivation and effective use of family habits of the heart.

Record family habits of the heart and any accompanying time commitments to carry them out:

CULTIVATING HABITS IN OUR CHURCH FAMILY
SESSION 4

So often today church is understood as a place to attend. Discipleship material is always careful to include a chapter on supporting your local church and your pastor. But, this whole way of thinking segments the church to a small part of our lives that we need to be sure to include, usually along with other community organizations and responsibilities. This way of thinking is completely foreign to the New Testament and very destructive to the process of establishing our lives on the first principles of the faith. We spent the entire second book of this series, *Becoming a Family of Families*, building the biblical framework that we are to be part of a local church community, and that community is to be a real extended family. But we need to go further. We need to think through the habits of involvement in the community that have to do with our growth in the faith and that of our families'. The first principles will never be fully incorporated into our lives in a vital way without genuinely building these habits into our lives. We will focus on a passage in Hebrews 10:23-25 to gain a foundation for these habits and then comment briefly on habits that build from it.

 ## Study the Scriptures

Read the Passage: Hebrews 10:23-25

Think Through the Questions:

1. What is "the confession of our hope"? What would it mean to waver in this confession?

2. What does it mean to stimulate one another when we are assembled together?

3. Why is it so important to assemble regularly with the church family?

Summarize the Core Teaching of the Passage:

Write a paragraph, outline, annotate, or chart your conclusions— whatever best communicates for you. Comment on why the habit of assembling together is an essential habit for a disciple.

Core teaching of Hebrews 10:23-25:

_____

_____

_____

_____

_____

_____

_____

_____

_____

_____

_____

_____

_____

_____

_____

_____

_____

_____

_____

Consult the Scholars

The following comments are designed to help you better understand the passage and to stimulate your thinking on the implications of the teaching.

Read and Reflect on this Brief Commentary on Hebrews 10:23-25:

Although this is just a small part of a larger passage, it is very important in understanding the basic heart habit that undergirds all of the other important community habits, which are directed to disciples of Jesus Christ. As always in Bible study, the context of Hebrews is critical to understanding the meaning of this text. An unknown author wrote this letter to the Jewish (i.e. Hebrew) believers who were experiencing such rejection by their Jewish extended families and communities that they were considering leaving their new faith in Christ and returning to the Jewish faith. This letter was written with the goal of encouraging these Jewish believers to remain steadfast in their faith in Christ. In the letter, there are a series of warnings to them about returning to the Jewish faith, since the Jewish nation was under the judgment of God for crucifying Christ. Jerusalem was about to be ransacked by Rome and the Jewish people were either killed or scattered among all the nations. All of this was foretold in Old Testament prophecy; they were the consequences of rejecting the Messiah—Jesus Christ. Hebrews is difficult to understand because it requires an extensive knowledge of the Old Testament, yet it presents a very extensive picture of the person and work of Christ. According to Hebrews 5:11-14, these are things to be pursued after you understand the first principles of the faith. Yet the core of some of the warnings are very clear. One such warning is our passage, Hebrews 10:23-25.

There are really only two commands in this section. The first is for them to hold to the "confession of their hope without wavering," 10:23. The confession here refers to their profession of belief in the faith, summarized in the teachings of Christ. The heart of this confession is the first principles of the faith (Hebrews 5:11-6:1). Some of the Jewish believers were beginning to waver because of intense persecution from their families and Jewish leaders. The second command is for believers to *stimulate* (literally, "to provoke a change in motivation or attitude") each other to stay with the faith and the life of love and good deeds that follows. He then exhorted them not to abandon assembling together as believers, referring to meetings of the local church communities. Some were habitually missing these regular meetings. Because of failing to take these meetings seriously and because of persecution from their Jewish families, from leaders of the Jewish synagogues, and from the nation, some were coming close to abandoning their faith.

Though most of us did not convert to Christ from Judaism, all of us who choose to become believers and be baptized are going to experience pressure from somewhere to abandon our faith, or at least not to continue on strongly. Thus we all need to assemble together with a local church community to be firmly established in our confession of the faith and to be encouraged to produce a life of love and good deeds, which is to accompany our salvation. As we have studied in the second book of this series, *Belonging to a Family of Families,* when we trust in Christ, we really are to become part of a believing family. At times, this may put pressure on us from our extended and immediate families. It is essential that we gather together with believers and become a vital part of the community life.

In our passage, we have seen the command for the habit of assembling together. As you read the letters of the early church leaders to the churches they founded, especially Paul's letters, you will find a lot of material on the habits of the community life of those churches. (You can study these passages in depth in the advanced, companion volume to this booklet, *Becoming Established in a Disciplined Lifestyle*, see page 69.) A brief survey of community habits of the heart are included here to help guide you as you reflect on the issue of cultivating church family habits and as you work on your project. The idea presented in the letters to the early churches is far larger than just habitually attending meetings of the church. They were to engage in those meetings in such a way that they became part of their habits of the heart. Here are a few of the directives:

- They were to constantly share the Word with one another—in psalms and hymns and spiritual songs. (Colossians 3:16)

- They were to each exercise their spiritual gifts and be faithful to the ministries that emerged from them. (1 Corinthians 12:4-6)

- They were to regularly observe the Lord's supper—a part of their assembling together. In New Testament times, this took place around a meal. (1 Corinthians 11:17-34)

- Each family, represented by the father at the assembly meeting, was to come prepared with something to share. (1 Corinthians 14:26-40)

These are just a few of the habits of the heart that we are to be exercising in the local church family. As you can see, our becoming established in the first principles of the faith and going on in the faith is not just a matter of exercising a few private, personal habits of the heart, but it is a disciplined life lived out in vital community life.

Read and Reflect on Key Quotes:

The following quote is taken from I. Howard Marshall's treatise on the Lord's Supper, entitled *Last Supper and Lord's Supper*. Marshall is an excellent early church scholar from England. The entire book is devoted to an early church study of the Lord's Supper. This quote is from the conclusion of his work.

"Following the intention of Jesus, whether implicit or as expressed in the command to repeat the action, the early church met together for fellowship meals which included this rite, known as the Breaking of Bread. In all probability these meals represented a continuation of the meals which the disciples, or rather the inner circle of them, had enjoyed with one another and with Jesus during his ministry. Since Jesus had appeared to them at mealtimes after his resurrection, the early Christians regarded their continuing meals together as occasions when Jesus himself was still present with them, though now unseen. At first such meals were held daily, and we do not know for certain whether the Breaking of Bread formed a part of the meal each time it was held or was celebrated less frequently. Nor do we know how long the church continued to meet daily in this way. Certainly by the time that 1 Corinthians was written we gain the impression that the Breaking of Bread was an integral part of the meal and that the meal was held on Sundays; the same impression can be drawn from Acts 20:7-11 which describes a scene roughly contemporary with that pictured in 1 Corinthians. There may have been a special feast associated with the annual Passover season in memory of the death and resurrection of Jesus.

"The Christian meals no doubt took differing forms from place to place and from time to time. Any attempt to provide a composite picture on the basis of the different pieces of evidence must consequently be resisted, but we can draw together the various items that were associated with the meal at one time or another. It is clear that such occasions normally included Christian instruction, together with prayers and the singing of hymns. There is some debate as to whether the Christians met for instruction and praise of this kind apart from their meetings to celebrate the Lord's Supper, but on the whole it is more probable that they did; the description of a Christian meeting in 1 Corinthians 14 gives the impression that it was a separate occasion from the church meal described earlier in the same letter. But there is no doubt that teaching was an integral part of the church meal. The extended teaching that followed the meal in Luke 22 and John 14-16 points in this direction. The endings of some of the Pauline letters and of the Revelation may have been phrased so as to lead on to the celebration of the Lord's Supper. . .

". . . It seems most likely that the order in Corinth was teaching, the Breaking of Bread, and the common meal, with the proviso that some members of the church were indulging their hunger and thirst before the start of the proceedings."[4]

The next quote is from Robert Bank's book, *Paul's Idea of Community: The Early House Churches in Their Historical Setting.* He has been influential in the house church movement in Australia and has done extensive research on the early churches of the New Testament and the couple of centuries following.

"Concerning the time and frequency of these early Christian meetings, Paul has little to say. He does request that contributions for the

Jerusalem collection be set aside 'on the first day of every week' (1 Cor 16:2). But this refers to an individual rather than communal action, as the words 'and store it up' indicate, and so does not necessarily allude to a weekly gathering. This expression, 'on the first day of every week' recurs in Luke's account of Paul's final meeting with the Christians in Troas (when all 'were gathered together to break bread,' Acts 20:7). But we cannot tell for certain whether the church regularly met on that day or had chosen it because of Paul's departure the following morning. If it is the former, as is more likely, we are still not clear whether the weekly meetings were of all the Christians or of the smaller groups. Paul's rather vague way of referring to meetings of the *whole* church suggests that it met less than once a week. Voluntary and cult associations met on a monthly basis; these larger Christian gatherings may well have followed suit.

"The Lucan passage describes a night meeting—understandable enough in view of the obligation upon most people to work during the day. Which evening is in view then? It is generally assumed that Luke had Sunday in mind. But it is more likely that it was on Saturday night that the Christians in Troas gathered together, the 'first day of the week' having begun at sunset (cf. NIV). Though in Pliny's time (first century AD) and area a Sunday night meeting took place, the evidence for when early Christians met is so slender that it would be unwise to make any confident generalizations. We are much more in the dark about the question than is commonly recognized.

"In these early letters of Paul, the term *ekklesia* consistently refers to actual gatherings of Christians as such, or to Christians in a local area conceived or defined as a regularly assembling community. This means that 'church' has a distinctly dynamic rather than static character. It is a regular occurrence rather than an ongoing reality. The word does not describe all the Christians who live in a particular locality if they do not gather. Nor does it refer to the sum total of Christians in a region or scattered throughout the world at any particular time. And never during this period is the term applied to the building in which Christians meet. Whether we are considering the smaller gatherings of only some Christians in a city or the larger meetings involving the whole Christian population, it is in the home of one of the members that *ekklesia* is held—for example in the 'upper room.' Not until the third century do we have evidence of special buildings being constructed for Christian gatherings and, even then, they were modeled on the room for receiving guests in the typical Roman and Greek household."[5]

45

Record any insights from the brief commentary and quotes:

Think Through the Issues

As we mentioned earlier, in our culture today we have reduced vital, dynamic involvement in the life of a local church community to "attending a church service." Most discipleship material spends lots of time focusing on all of our individual habits but only gives a token nod to the local church. For example, we are encouraged to take our turn serving in some ministry or serving a term on the church board. But the local church community nowhere resembles the community life of the early churches. The Lord's Supper has been reduced from a community meal containing significant community ministry to a token ritual tacked on at the end of a service. Gone is the expectation of each believer coming together to minister the Word to each other out of real sharing and relationships. In this issue, we will examine the importance of becoming deeply and habitually involved in the life of a local church community and the impact which that involvement plays in becoming fully established in our faith.

Issue: Importance of church community habits of the heart

Think Through the Issue Before Discussion:

1. What is the difference between "attending church" in our token cultural fashion and assembling with a local church family in the fashion of the early churches?

2. Following the New Testament example, what are some of the heart habits that need to be part of a local church community?

3. How important are these habits to integrating the first principles fully into our lives? Into the lives of our families?

4. What do you think is the relationship between building our lives around the first principles of the faith and vital involvement in the life of a local church family?

Record your initial thoughts on the issue before discussion:

Discuss the issue in your small group.

Record your final thoughts on the issue after discussion:

_____

_____

_____

_____

_____

_____

_____

_____

_____

_____

_____

_____

_____

_____

_____

_____

_____

_____

Apply the Principles

It is now time to respond to what you have studied and discussed. Take your time on this section.

Think Back Through the First Three Steps.

Whether you are from a churched or unchurched background, these ideas may be very new to you. As mentioned in the introduction of this booklet, those of us from a Western culture, especially American, live in an individualistic society—pursuing our own goals, our own development, and our own spirituality. We know very little about true community and even less about the habits of the heart that need to be intertwined with true community. We have to rethink the foundations of our lives.

Design an Application for Your Life.

Think through the process of becoming vitally involved in a local church community. How does God intend your personal habits to be intertwined with the life of a local church community? What are the habits that must be in your life to be a vital part of a local church community? What are the core community habits you need to develop? Record your thoughts below.

List the core "habits" required for full involvement in the life of a local church community. Then record your thoughts about how your life needs to change in order to become vitally involved in a local church family.

CULTIVATING HABITS IN YOUR LIFEWORK
SESSION 5

We have a tendency to separate our lives as disciples of Christ from the world around us, especially our work lives. We are inventing a term in this series—*lifework*—to help us avoid this problem from the very beginning and to develop an understanding of a very exciting and thoroughly biblical concept. The idea of *lifework* is much bigger than just our paid work. It includes our paid work, of course, but also our family work, our home work, our non-paid work, our work in service to others, work for our church family, and work that is specially related to our gifts and calling. Obviously, these are all intertwined. Together they make up our *lifework*—the complete work of our lives to which God has called us (Ephesians 2:10). There are many disciplines—*habits of the heart*—to which we must be committed to completely fulfill our lifework. In this session, we will focus on the most foundational discipline of our lifework—a good, sound work ethic. It is foundational for Christians who are building their lives around the first principles of the philosophy of Christ. We will study 1 Thessalonians 4:9-12, a text on work that Paul directly ties in with becoming established in the faith.

 Study the Scriptures

Read the Passage: 1 Thessalonians 4:9-12

Think Through the Questions:

1. In this passage, what does it mean to "behave properly toward outsiders and not be in any need"?

2. According to this passage, what does it mean to be in need?

3. He urges them to lead a certain lifestyle here and implies that they should avoid the opposite lifestyle. What are the two lifestyles?

4. Are we all supposed to be doing manual labor? If not, what does it mean when he says to "work with your hands"?

Summarize the Core Teaching of the Passage:

Write a paragraph, outline, annotate, or chart your conclusions—whatever best communicates for you. Be sure to comment on the work ethic or discipline that is to be normative for all Christians.

Core teaching of 1 Thessalonians 4:9-12:

Consult the Scholars

The following comments are designed to help you better understand the passage and to stimulate your thinking on the implications of the teaching.

Read and Reflect on this Brief Commentary on
1 Thessalonians 4:9-12:

Paul wrote two letters to the Thessalonica church, both for the purpose of more fully establishing the young church in the gospel. As with all of the churches, almost as soon as he completed his initial work with them and left them, someone came in to undermine his teaching or to upset the church, getting it off track somehow. Three problems were affecting the church: sexual immorality, a failure by some to work, and a distorted teaching about the return of Christ, which was brought in by outsiders. Our passage is the first of two parts of Paul's instructions to the Thessalonians concerning the importance of living a disciplined lifestyle and a warning against an irresponsible lifestyle. The first passage is 1 Thessalonians 4:9-12, and the follow-up conversation on the issue is given in his second letter to the Thessalonians, in 3:6-15. Taken together, we get a clearer picture of exactly what Paul was saying. We will just examine the first passage but allude to the second as needed to shed light on the first.

Paul gave a very simple directive to the church, which we need to examine carefully. The directive was essentially to lead a quiet life, to focus on their own business, and to work with their hands. What exactly did he mean by this? To understand it, we must understand the problem he was addressing. According to 2 Thessalonians 3:6-15, some were unwilling to work. In addition, they were meddling in others' lives. Evidently they were claiming that, as Christians, others should support them, since they were brothers—brothers evidently too valuable to do basic labor with their hands. Paul said that these believers were living undisciplined lifestyles, going against his teaching. If they did not listen, the church was to disassociate from them.

This helps us gain full insight into what he commanded in 1 Thessalonians 4:9-12. When he told the Thessalonians to "lead a quiet life and attend to your own business" (4:11), he was telling them to avoid the example of those who were getting into everyone else's business and yet failing to be responsible for their own work. It also implies, as explained in the Malherbe quote below, that their lives were to be marked by responsible and successful work from which would come effective ministry, rather than by an activist lifestyle, which tries to make an impact through political causes. The phrase "work with your hands" is a phrase that simply means that they were all to work and provide for themselves, not to be lazy and expect others to provide for them. They were all to be characterized by a disciplined work ethic. This is one of the very first disciplines (and a first principle itself) for how we are to live and work in the world as Christians. This kind of *lifestyle* ("behave" in 4:12, literally means "walk," the same term used in Ephesians 4:1) is to mark all Christians.

Is this command authoritative? Is a disciplined work ethic really part of the first principles of the faith? Yes, Paul makes this very clear in his letters to the Thessalonians. In 2 Thessalonians 2:15, the church was to "hold to the traditions" they were taught in the letter. The term *traditions* literally means "authoritative teaching passed down by the Apostles," by letter or by direct teaching. Anyone who did not listen to this teaching ("tradition," 2 Thessalonians 3:6) was to be corrected and eventually disassociated with until he repented and conformed to it. 1 Thessalonians 4:1-2 states that these instructions about how they were supposed to walk were given by the authority of Jesus Christ. It was clearly part of the disciplined lifestyle of every believer. It was part of the first principles of the teachings of Jesus Christ.

This work ethic directive is actually a habit of the heart as well. This can be seen by the fact that it requires daily disciplined work characterized by an accompanying attitude. It is clear that this disciplined approach also applies to anyone preparing for work that will allow him to provide for himself, whether an apprenticeship or getting an education. From this grows a whole set of lifework disciplines. One that we have already seen in Titus 3:12-14 is that we should engage in good occupations. In our society, another that becomes necessary is an orientation of lifelong learning—another habit of the heart. We will look at these and others in coming booklets. But at the foundation of a disciplined lifestyle is a habit of responsible, disciplined work.

Read and Reflect on Key Quotes:

The following quote is from Abraham Malherbe's work entitled *Paul and the Thessalonians*. Malherbe is probably the best-known, contemporary early church scholar. He teaches at Yale Divinity School. This quote is not easy to follow without a brief summary of the context, but it is the very best research on 1 Thessalonians 4:11-12. It helps us gain a clear sense of what Paul was really encouraging the Thessalonians in. Malherbe's main argument centers on the idea that while Paul was encouraging them to live quiet lives, the point was not to become an elitist withdrawn society (as some philosophers of his day encouraged). But they needed to live model lives of stability resulting from their good work ethic; this would be a more effective means of impacting the world than political activism.

"So far we have concentrated on Paul's efforts to ensure that the Thessalonians continued to grow as individuals within their Christian community. Paul does not, however, only direct their attention inward. Groups such as the Thessalonians could not exist without defining their relationship to the larger society. Thus 1 Thessalonians exhibits an interest in how the recently converted Christians were to conduct themselves toward outsiders. The Thessalonians' social conduct was of the greatest importance to Paul, so much so that he reserves admonition for those who are disorderly (5:14). . . .

"Paul gives his most explicit instruction regarding the need for Christians to lead a quiet life in 1 Thess. 4:9-12: . . .

"Like the other two places where he encourages a positive attitude toward non-Christians (3:11-12; 5:15), this passage begins with a reference to love within the community but concludes with a statement on the purpose of Paul's advice—'so that you may command the respect of outsiders, and be dependent on nobody.' . . .

"The items clearly derived from such discussions are his instructions: that his readers aspire to live quietly, that they mind their own affairs, and that they be self-sufficient (literally, 'and have need of no one,' or 'of nothing'). The contrast between being meddlesome or being a busybody and living quietly and minding one's own affairs had frequently been taken up in discussions about Greek social and political values before Plato. Plato himself commended the person who 'remains quiet (*hēsychazein*) and minds his own affairs (*ta hautou prattein*),' and characterized justice as minding one's own business and not being a meddler or busybody (*polypragmonein*). The expression 'to remain quiet and mind one's own business' came to describe the person who withdrew from the political arena, particularly in the late Roman Republic and early Empire, when renunciation of public life was a particularly attractive choice for thoughtful people. . . .

"These examples demonstrate that the language Paul uses to instruct the Thessalonians in social responsibility was commonly used in the first century to describe the contemplative life in opposition to an activism that was described as meddlesomeness (*polypragmosyne*). There are obvious differences, however, between Paul and these philosophers. Where Paul resembles the Stoics and persons like Chion is in his command to the Thessalonians 'to live quietly' and 'to mind your own affairs.' Where he differs is in his expectation that by so doing his readers would meet with the approval of non-Christians ('outsiders,' 1 Thess. 4:12). . . . Finally, Paul's concentration on manual labor and self-sufficiency shows that he is concerned with Christian behavior on the economic and social levels rather than on the political level, as was primarily the case with the philosophers we have so far encountered.

"Paul's own labor was paradigmatic when he established the church; it is referred to in 1 Thess. 2:9 where it provides the basis for his exhortation to the Thessalonians to work, and it occurs again in 2 Thessalonians.

"This context, in which the newly converted abandoned their trades and took to the streets, helps to explain Paul's preoccupation with his own and his converts' employment. Aware of the criticism by members of polite society that such persons were disgraceful and socially irresponsible, busybodies who meddled in the affairs of others, Paul offered a contrary example in his own life. Whether or not this was the reason why he centered his activity in the workshop in the first place cannot be determined. That he did so, however, enabled him to be more forceful in his directions. By giving his instructions in terms that had come to be used of philosophers who sought a higher good by living quietly and avoiding meddlesomeness, Paul implicitly distanced Christians from the socially irresponsible Cynics.

"There is yet another difference between Paul's directions and the situation of those retirement-seeking philosophers described so far in this chapter. Chion retired in the company of a friend, but none of the others emphasize such an association or make any mention of a community of kindred souls. Paul, by contrast, considers his directions to fall under the heading of brotherly love (1 Thess. 4:9), that is, the special relationship within the Christian community. He uses the term 'brotherly love' (*philadelphia*) only once elsewhere, in Rom. 12:10, where he instructs his readers to be affectionate toward one another in brotherly love. That he has in mind more than mere affection, however, appears from Rom. 12:13, in the same context: 'Contribute to the needs of the saints, practice hospitality.'"[6]

Record any insights from the brief commentary and quotes:

Think Through the Issues

We cannot gain a sense of our lifework, let alone develop an effective witness in the world, if we have not developed a disciplined work ethic. If we do not have disciplined work habits, we will probably not provide well for our families and may find ourselves in need of assistance. Consequently, as disciples of Christ, it is very difficult to expect to gain an audience from the watching world as we share about our Master. He Himself worked as a carpenter. Discuss this issue as a group, making sure to note the relationship of a disciplined work ethic to our witness as disciples.

Issue: Importance of disciplined work habits of the heart

Think Through the Issue Before Discussion:

1. Why is an outstanding work ethic such a powerful witness to the watching world?

2. Should this really be a first principle of the faith? Should it be so important that we would eventually disassociate from a believer who will not work? Why?

3. What exactly is the habit or habits of the heart here? How do these habits apply to one who is in school, or an apprentice, or a teenager?

4. Why do you think Christians so readily disassociate their work from their faith?

Record your initial thoughts on the issue before discussion:

Discuss the issue in your small group.

Record your final thoughts on the issue after discussion:

Apply the Principles

It is now time to respond to what you have studied and discussed. Take your time on this section.

Think Back Through the First Three Steps.

Think back through your life up to this point. In one sense, you inherit your work ethic from your parents. Regardless of where you are in life, would you say your life is characterized by a good work ethic? Reflect on how your life squares with 1 Thessalonians 4:11-12.

Design an Application for Your Life.

Think through the actual habits of the heart of one who has a disciplined work ethic—of one who is building his life on the first principles of Christ. Then describe why these are important—to our families, to the local church community, and before the watching world.

List the habits of one who has a disciplined work ethic. Describe the importance of this to our lives as disciples of Jesus Christ:

RESHAPING OUR LIVES
SESSION 6

It is now time to pull together all of our applications from the first five sessions, in order to affect our whole lives. In this fast-paced world, it is hard to find time to do any serious reflection. While we have benefited from the exercises in the first five sessions, actually integrating the truths into our lives as a whole takes extra effort. Taken together, they can become a powerful force bringing about significant change—change designed to reshape our lives.

As in all of the other booklets, session six is designed to pull it all together. This is especially helpful in this booklet, since the very intent of the booklet is to build an integrated set of life habits. These habits are designed to move the knowledge we have learned in the first three booklets fully into our hearts, that we might completely grasp (and therefore fully live) the magnificent plan that God has set before our lives and families. In addition, this session goes a long way toward integrating all of our work from the first four booklets.

 ## Committing Your Heart
Reflection, Personal Journaling, and Prayer

Journaling is an excellent way to reflect more deeply about the significance of what we have been learning. It forces us to express in words what has entered our hearts. It helps us identify and clarify what the Spirit has been using in the Word to enlighten our hearts, as well as to convict us. Prayer should follow this. We should ask God to permanently transform our hearts to give us a desire and a longing to grow to maturity.

In this section, think back over your work from each of the five previous sessions. What happened in your life because of your work in each session? Record your thoughts, and reflect on what you wrote. What new convictions have you developed? What have you seen God begin to do in your life? Are there areas that you wish you had followed through on more fully? What affected you most? What convicted you most? What excited you most? How has your philosophy of life changed?

Finally, formulate these thoughts into one main prayer request. If you were to ask God to give you the ability to live a disciplined lifestyle, how would you ask it? What habits of the heart would you ask to become heart convictions first? Write the request in a paragraph. Transfer it to a 3- x 5-inch card and carry it with you. Pray over it regularly. Over the next few weeks, record on the back of the card any ways that you see God answering your prayer.

Your Journal — thoughts on developing a disciplined lifestyle:

Prayer Request:

Committing Your Mind
Forming Clear Convictions and Memorizing Scripture

It is essential that we pull together what we have studied—formulating our thoughts into clear convictions. What exactly does it mean to develop an integrated set of *life habits*? It is critical that we think clearly about the truths of Scripture. If we have wrong ideas in our heads, then our lives will be built on those wrong foundations. If we misunderstand what it means to grow in our faith, our whole lives may be set on a wrong course. We may develop study habits that are based on experience and are merely individualistic. Our faith may not be integrated into our lifestyle: giving just a token nod to the church by just attending or taking our turn to serve; our families may not catch the faith; and our work may be separated from our faith.

Begin by summarizing your studies concerning the process of developing a disciplined lifestyle into one paragraph—ideally bringing together all of the important truths that you studied in the five sessions. Then, list the essential Bible references to back up your convictions. Finally, choose at least one of these verses to memorize, record it below, and quote it by memory to your study group when you meet. Transfer it to a 3- x 5-inch card—writing the verse(s) and reference on one side and your insights into the verse(s) on the other side. Review it for about six weeks.

Profile of a disciplined lifestyle—core convictions:

Key verse to memorize:

Committing Your Life

Decisions, Personal Projects, and Life Habits

Think back over the "Apply the Principles" section of each of the five sessions. It is one thing to think about specific applications to our lives as we move through each study. It is another thing to think across our whole lives and begin reshaping our life goals and our lifestyles by what we are learning. This is a vital part of building our lives around the first principles of Christ rather than around the first principles of the world.

Several things are necessary in order to integrate these principles into our lives. First, look back over your "Apply the Principles" sections and your work so far in this session. Are there decisions that you need to make? For example, are there life habits that you have been living that you need to change in light of this study? Are there personal projects that come to your mind that would help you develop a disciplined lifestyle? An excellent project would be to develop an integrated set of disciplines in each of the four areas of life—individual, family, local church family, and lifework—built from your study in this book. Then design a plan for building these habits into your life. Share these plans with a spouse, parent, or trusted believer for encouragement and accountability.

Decisions, personal projects, and life habits:

Endnotes

[1] Ray C. Stedman, *Our Riches in Christ* (Grand Rapids, Michigan: Discovery House Publishers, 1998) pp. 211-213. All rights reserved; used by permission of the publisher.

[2] Francis A. Schaeffer, *True Spirituality* (Wheaton, Illinois: Tyndale House Publishers, 1971) pp. 120-122. Used by permission of the publisher.

[3] Stephen B. Clark, *Man and Woman in Christ: An Examination of the Roles of Men and Women in Light of Scripture and the Social Sciences* (Ann Arbor: Servant Books, 1990) pp. 68-69. Used by permission of the author.

[4] I. Howard Marshall, *Last Supper and Lord's Supper* (Grand Rapids, Michigan: William B. Eerdman's Publishing Company, 1980) pp. 144-145. Used by permission of Paternoster Press.

[5] Robert Banks, *Paul's Idea of Community: The Early House Churches in Their Historical Setting* (Grand Rapids, Michigan: William B. Eerdman's Publishing Company, 1980) pp. 40-41. Used by permission of the publisher.

[6] Abraham Malherbe, *Paul and the Thessalonians* (Philadelphia: Fortress Press, 1987) pp. 95-102. Used by permission of the author.

Glossary of Key Biblical Terms and Concepts

The following is a list of important terms that you may have encountered for the first time in this study. Although they are explained in the booklet, it is easy to forget their exact meanings. This glossary can also serve as a catalogue of biblical terms and concepts for future reference.

Assembly Meeting. The meetings of the early churches were called assembly meetings. They were built around the concept of the church being a family. Everyone was encouraged to participate. The men were to represent their families as the Word was taught and debated. Everyone shared in the Lord's Supper, which in the first century usually included a meal. They all spoke to one another in "psalms and hymns and spiritual songs." Today, in the West, we have replaced the New Testament assembly meeting with a formal church service. Acts 20:7-12; 1 Corinthians 12-14.

Devotions. A contemporary term for spending time with God daily, especially reading the Bible and praying. Other terms for this idea include *quiet time* and *time in the Word*. These terms are used for the core of the spiritual disciplines.

Discipline and Instruction. Two terms used by Paul in Ephesians 6:4 to represent the entire training process for which parents, especially fathers, are responsible for their children. The first word, *discipline* (literally "paideia"), refers to the general educational process; and the second word, *instruction*, carries the idea of building solid minds, including the discipline needed to shape those minds.

Enlightenment, The. A period of history covering the last several hundred years when scientific method dominated all ways of interpreting reality. Mankind is now beginning to recognize the limits of science and a new Post-Enlightenment age is beginning to emerge.

Enlightenment. Eastern enlightenment is a spiritual philosophy. It encourages its adherents to empty themselves of all thought and to try to attain a totally pure state, in which one can get in touch with creation, and through that purity, to reach a tranquil, enlightened state.

Enlightenment is also a biblical concept taught by Paul in which a person gradually comes to fully understand all that they have in Christ. Becoming enlightened comes through a study of, and a reflection on, the true knowledge and through the work of the Spirit in our hearts. Ephesians 1:15-23; 3:14-21.

Habits of the Heart. A phrase used to represent a whole series of inward life disciplines that need to be developed as disciples of Jesus Christ. They encompass all areas of our lives: personal, family, church community, and world.

Lifestyle. A whole way of life, a way that affects every area of life: individual goals and aspirations, family life, community life, and work. We are using it in this book as a synonym for what Paul called our *walk*, our way of life. Ephesians 4:1.

Lifework. A term created for this series that refers to the total work of our lives, including paid work, volunteer work, work at home, etc. Each of us should develop a clearer and clearer understanding of the work God has created for us to do as we mature, understand our gifts, and respond to life's presenting opportunities. Ephesians 2:10.

Lord's Supper. The practice of the early church in which the entire church assembly focused on what Christ had done for them on the cross. The two main elements of the ceremony included the breaking of bread (the loaf symbolized Christ's broken body on the cross, which enabled believers to become one family) and taking the cup (the cup symbolized Christ's blood, which was shed to cover their sins). Both Christ and Paul commanded the believers to observe the Lord's Supper. It is called Communion by some churches today and the Eucharist by others. 1 Corinthians 11:17-34.

Paideia. See "Discipline and Instruction."

Quiet Life. Paul's concept of the quiet life was different from the Greek philosophers of his day and the monks of medieval times. In the New Testament, a quiet life refers to one who remains active in community life but rather than joining causes and political agendas, establishes a powerful witness by skillful and successful work and faithfully providing for his own family. 1 Thessalonians 4:9-12.

Spiritual Disciplines. Over the centuries, this phrase has become the common term used to represent a whole set of individual disciplines that the Christian exercises in order to grow spiritually or to strengthen his personal relationship with God. Spiritual disciplines traditionally include such practices as prayer, meditation, reading the Bible, journaling, fasting, etc.

Lifelong Learning

The booklets of this series are designed to lay the very essential foundations of the faith. They are intended to be just a beginning. The writer of the New Testament letter, Hebrews, reminds us that we are to move on to maturity (Hebrews 5:11-14). This Lifelong Learning section is at the end of each First Principles Series booklet. It will serve as a guide to some of the resources that will enable you to build solidly on the foundations laid in each booklet and, therefore, urge you to press on toward maturity. Review these resources and include any that you would like to read or work through in the "Committing Your Life" section of the sixth session.

1. The First Principles—Series Two

Series Two is a follow-up to the series you have just completed. The first series focused on the first principles of our faith as a whole, giving special attention to life in the household of faith—a local church community. This next series narrows the focus to individual households. Book one begins examining the marriage relationship of a disciple. Book two looks at how to pass on our faith—the first principles—to our children. Book three revisits the whole concept of our lifework. And book four focuses on turning our households into intergenerational heritage.

2. The First Principles—Series Three

Series Three is a follow-up to Series One and Two. The first two series focus on a complete study of the first principles of the faith. This last series revisits the first principles and strengthens our understanding of them by studying Acts and several of the New Testament letters in which they appear. In book one, we will learn a natural method for accurately interpreting the Scriptures. In book two, we will study the entire book of Acts. In books three through five, we will study Paul's early letters (1 & 2 Thessalonians), a middle letter (Ephesians), and three later letters (the Pastoral Epistles). This will greatly strengthen our grasp of the first principles of the faith.

3. *Going to Church in the First Century*, by Robert Banks (Christian Books Publishing House)

This is an often-unknown booklet of only 48 pages by one who has been closely involved in the development of house churches in Australia. It is a brief narrative depicting what is was like going to church in the first century. It is helpful to read because we are so stuck in our "church service" paradigm of the West that it is almost impossible to envision what the New Testament church was really like. It is a very useful supplement to this First Principles booklet, especially session four.